THE QUEST FOR FRUIT

By

R.L. PITTS

www.rlpitts.com

Library of Congress Cataloging-in-Publication Data

Identifier: ISBN: 979-8-218-97812-9

Names: R.L. Pitts

Title: The Quest for Fruit

Description: First Edition

Subject: Inspirational and adventurous fiction.

My books may be purchased in bulk for promotional, educational, or business use.

Please contact your local bookseller or rl@rlpitts.com.

First edition 2024

Edited by Janice Pitts

For my grandson, Ari Jae

Also, by R.L. Pitts

The Murderacracy

Of Fury and Faith

Hustle Summer (Out of print)

Table of Contents

THE QUEST FOR FRUIT

Prologue

When Bayboo was a young boy, he lived in a small village in the mountains where he spent his days exploring nature and learning new things. He was always kind and helpful to everyone he met, even plants and animals. He believed that besides love, kindness was the most powerful force in the world, and that giving it could make anyone happy.

One day, he decided to go on a quest to find the source of kindness. He wanted to see where it came from and how it spread. He packed his bag with some food, water, and a map, and set off on his journey. He followed the river that flowed through the village and down the mountain, hoping that it would lead him to the kindness spring.

Along the way he met many challenges and dangers. He had to cross a raggedy bridge across a gorge, climb a steep cliff with sharp rocks, and avoid a hungry bear that was looking for a snack. But he also met many friends and allies. He helped a lost bird find its way back to its nest, shared his food with a hungry squirrel, and sang a song with a cheerful frog. He learned something new from each of them and they thanked him for his kindness.

He also met some people who were not so kind. He met a greedy merchant who tried to trick him into buying a fake map, a rude traveler who pushed him aside on the road, and a mean bully who mocked him for his quest. But he did not let it discourage him or make him angry. He responded with kindness and compassion, hoping it would change their ways.

After many days of traveling, he finally reached the end of the river. He saw a beautiful waterfall that sparkled in the sunlight. He climbed up to the top of the waterfall and looked around. He saw a small pool of clear water that was surrounded by flowers and trees. He felt a warm and gentle breeze caress his face. A soft and soothing voice rode in on the wind and whispered in his ear.

"Welcome, Bayboo. You have found the Source of Kindness."

He was delighted and amazed. He had completed his quest. He asked the voice who it was and where it came from.

"I am Kindness, itself," the voice said., "I come from within you and everyone who has a kind heart. I flow through the river of life and touch everything that lives. I am everywhere and nowhere at the same time."

Bayboo was confused and curious. He asked the voice how he could see it and talk to it.

"You can see me and talk to me because you have been kind to everyone on your journey," the voice said. "You have shown me your true self and I have shown you mine. You have earned my trust and friendship."

Bayboo felt honored and grateful. He asked the voice what he could do to thank it and show his appreciation?

"You don't have to do anything more than you've already done," the voice said. "You have given me the greatest gift of all, your kindness. Just keep being yourself and spreading kindness wherever you go. That is all I ask of you."

Bayboo smiled and nodded. He thanked the voice for its wisdom and guidance and said goodbye. He filled his bottle with water from the pool as a souvenir of his quest. He then turned around and started making his way back to his village.

He knew his adventures were not over yet. He still had many things to learn and many people to meet. But he also knew that he had found something precious and priceless: the Source of Kindness. He hoped that one day everyone would find it, too.

I

Kindness

Over time Bayboo's village grew surrounded by the mountains where he lived with his grandson Erasto, and their dog Tashi. They loved each other and enjoyed spending time together. By this time, Bayboo's reputation had grown, and he was highly respected by all. One day, Bayboo decided to take Erasto and Tashi on a special adventure. He said, "Erasto, today we are going on a kindness quest. A long time ago the Source of Kindness gave me this map to look for opportunities to help others and spread kindness in all the villages that we know."

Curious and excited, Erasto asked, "Bayboo, what is a kindness quest? And how do we do it?"

Bayboo smiled and said, "A kindness quest is when we look for people or animals who need our help or could use some cheering up. With this map we do it by being observant, compassionate, and generous. We can also use our creativity and imagination to find ways to make someone's day better. With the way things are around here it will do everyone some good."

Erasto nodded and said, "That sounds like fun. Let's go!"

Tashi barked, "Woof, woof," in agreement, and wagged his tail.

Bayboo took Erasto's hand, and they walked out of their house with Tashi on a leash. The sun set high in the bright cloudless sky, and a gentle breeze ruffled the leaves on the hardwood trees. They walked east toward the park, where they hoped to find some opportunities to show kindness.

As they walked, they saw a lady carrying heavy bags of groceries. She looked tired and stressed. Bayboo said, "Erasto, look at that lady. She is having a tough time with her groceries. Do you think we can help her?"

Erasto said, "Yes Bayboo. Let's ask if she needs a hand?"

They approached the lady gently and offered to carry her bags for her. The lady was surprised and grateful. A light brightened her bespeckled eyes and she said, "Thank you so much. You are truly kind." She smiled and thanked them again as they put the groceries in her car.

As the continued their walk they approached a boy sitting on a bench. He looked sad and lonely. Bayboo said, "Erasto, look at that boy. He is feeling down. Do you think we can cheer him up?"

"Yes, Bayboo. Let's talk to him and see if he wants to play with us."

They came nearer to the pitiful youth and introduced themselves. They asked his name and why he was sad.

"My name is Tommy," said the boy. "And I am sad because I don't have any friends at school. Everyone thinks I'm weird because I like to read books and play chess."

"Well, Tommy," Bayboo said, "we think you are impressive because you like to read books and play chess. Those are great hobbies that makes you smart and interesting. We would love to be your friends."

Erasto said, "Yeah, Tommy. You aren't weird at all. Bayboo plays chess all the time. You are just unique, and we like you just the way you are." They invited Tommy to join them in their kindness quest and to play with Tashi who barked, "Woof, woof," and wagged his tail. Tommy smiled and agreed as he and Erasto played catch with Tashi.

After leaving Tommy, they continued their walk and happened upon a bird with a broken wing, lying in the grass. As they came closer, they could hear it cooing and looking scared. Bayboo said, "Erasto, look at that bird. It is in pain. Do you think we can help it?"

"Yes, Bayboo." Erasto said. "Let's take it to a veterinarian or to the animal shelter."

They carefully picked up the bird and Bayboo wrapped it in a handkerchief from his pocket. They asked around for the nearest vet or animal shelter. Someone pointed to one nearby and they took the injured bird there. The shelter staff thanked them for bringing the bird and promised that they would take loving care of it.

They continued their walk and spotted a homeless man flashing a sign at passing cars that said, "Anything helps." He looked sad and depressed when no one stopped.

"Erasto, look at that man," Bayboo said. "He looks tired, cold, and hungry. Do you think we can help him?"

"Yes, Bayboo," Erasto said. "Let's go buy him something to eat and drink and a blanket to keep him warm."

They went to a nearby market and bought sandwiches, bottled water, and a blanket. They gave them to the man and wished him well. The man thanked them sincerely and called them "Angels."

They continued their walk and saw a girl selling lemonade at a stand. She looked bored and disappointed. Bayboo said, "Erasto, look at that girl. She is trying to raise money for something important, but no one is buying her lemonade. Do you think we can help her?"

"Yes, Bayboo. Let's go and buy some lemonade from her and tell others about her stand," Erasto said.

They went to the girl's stand and bought some lemonade from her. They asked what she was raising money for, and she said she was raising money for a new bike because hers was stolen last week.

"That's unfortunate," Bayboo said, but it is very admirable of you to work hard to reach your goal."

"Yeah, that's very impressive. And your lemonade is delicious," Erasto said as he wiped his lips with the back of his hand. Tashi barked and wagged his tail.

They complimented her on her stand and sign and encouraged her to keep up her excellent work. Then to her surprise, they jumped in to help her by holding up the sign directing passersby to buy some lemonade. The girl was happy and grateful. "Thank you very much. You are exceedingly kind," she told them.

Further along their walk there was a woman sitting on a bench crying. She looked heartbroken and helpless.

"Erasto, look at that woman. She is going through a tough time. Do you think we can help her?" Bayboo asked.

"Yes, Bayboo. Let's talk to her and see if we can make her feel better," Erasto said. They approached the woman and asked if she was okay.

"No, I'm not okay," she said. "I just found out my husband cheated on me with my best friend. I don't know what to do. I feel like my life is over."

"We're sorry to hear that," Bayboo said. "that's a terrible thing to happen to anyone. You don't deserve that."

"Yeah, that's awful." Erasto said. "You deserve better than that. You deserve to be happy and loved." They offered words of comfort and encouragement. They told her that she was strong and beautiful and that she would get through this. Erasto gave her a flower he had picked from the park and said she had a lovely smile. Feeling better, the woman thanked them for their kindness and said they made her feel better and walked away holding the flower close to her heart.

They continued their walk and saw a man playing a guitar on the street corner. He was talented and enthusiastic, but no one paid him any attention or gave him any tips.

"Erasto, look at that man. He's a great musician, but no one appreciates his music. Do you think we can help him?" Bayboo asked.

"Yes, Bayboo. Let's listen to his music and give him a tip," Erasto said.

They stopped at the man's corner and admired the passion in his music. They clapped, cheered, and whistled after each song and put money in the hat sitting next to the guitar case. During a break they asked him about his music and his dreams. He man told them that he loved making music and wanted to be a famous singer and songwriter one day, but had found little success in the music industry, so far.

"I love making music, too," Bayboo said. "You play with such passion. Don't give up on your dreams," he encouraged him. "Just keep working hard and loving what you do and never give up on yourself."

"Yeah, like Bayboo said, don't lose hope," Erasto said. "Look around, you have many fans here who love your music," Erasto said, as a small crowd burst into spontaneous applause. "And others will appreciate it, too," he added.

They suggested some ways to promote his music online and offline and told him to stay connected to them. The man thanked them for their kindness and support and declared they were his biggest fans and supporters.

They continued their walk and saw a group of kids playing soccer in a field. They looked happy and energetic, but they had no proper equipment nor uniforms.

"Look at those kids, Erasto," Bayboo said. "Do you think we can help them?"

"Yes, Bayboo," Erasto said. "Let's go buy them some soccer balls, shoes, socks, jerseys, and nets." They went to a sporting goods store nearby and bought soccer items for the kids. When they returned to the field and gave it to them the kids were ecstatic and grateful. They said, "Thank you so much for your kindness and generosity." They invited Bayboo, Erasto, and Tashi to join in their game.

They played soccer with the kids for awhile and had lots of fun. They laughed. They cheered. They high fived each other. They made new friends and learned new skills.

After the game, they decided to end the kindness quest for the day. They said goodbye to their new friends and headed home. On their way home they reflected on their kindness quest. Erasto said, "I feel great, Bayboo. I'm happy and proud of us for helping so many people today."

Bayboo said, "Me, too, Erasto. I am so happy, too, and so proud of you for being such a kind-hearted boy."

"Woof, woof, woof," Tashi barked in agreement.

Bayboo asked, "Erasto, what did you learn from our kindness quest?"

"I learned that kindness is easy and fun to do. I learned that kindness makes others happy, but also makes us happy, too," Erasto said.

"That's right, Erasto. Kindness is a win-win for everyone involved," Bayboo said.

"Erasto, do you want to go on another kindness quest tomorrow? Bayboo asked.

"Yes, Bayboo. I want to do more kindness quests every day," Erasto laughed.

"Me, too," Bayboo laughed.

"Have you gone on other quests, Bayboo?" Erasto asked.

II

Love

Bayboo, Erasto, and Tashi had successfully completed their quest for kindness. They helped many people along the way, and learned about compassion, generosity, and gratitude. They were proud of themselves, but also curious about what else they could do to make the world a better place.

They decided to visit the Source of Kindness, who had given Bayboo the map for his first quest. They hoped the Source would have some advice for them, or another map to guide them.

They found the Source as a voice blowing in the wind, reading a book. He stopped reading aloud when he heard them approach. "Hello my friends," he greeted them warmly. "I see that you have returned from your quest. How did it go?"

It was amazing," Bayboo exclaimed. "We helped many people and made new friends, too."

"We learned about kindness and how it makes a difference in people's lives," Erasto added.

"And you had a lot of fun along the way, right boy?" Bayboo said.

"Woof," Tashi barked, wagging his tail.

The voice laughed. "I am happy to hear that. You have done well, my children. You have shown great courage and wisdom in your journey."

"But we're not done yet," Bayboo said. "We want to do more. We want to spread more kindness in the world."

"Is there another quest we can go on?" Erasto eagerly asked.

"Or another map you can give us?" Bayboo wondered.

The voice gave it some thought as the wind raised, gently, "Well, there is one more thing you can do, my friends. One more thing that can make the world a better place."

"What is it?" they asked eager to learn the answer.

With a twinkle in its tone the voice said, "It is the most powerful thing of all. It is the thing that can heal any wound, overcome any obstacle, and create any miracle. It is the thing that can unite all living beings in peace and harmony. It is the thing that can make you genuinely happy."

"What is it?" Erasto asked, more excited than ever.

Bayboo smiled and said, "It is love."

"Yes love. Bayboo is right, Erasto. Love is the ultimate quest. The greatest gift you can give and receive. Love is the essence of life itself," the voice said.

Bayboo nodded his head.

"But what is love?" Erasto asked, puzzled. "And how do we find it?"

The voice spoke softly, "Love is not something you find. Love is something you create. Love is something you express. Love is something you are."

It pulled a heart shaped pendant out of the air and gave it to Bayboo.

"This is the symbol of love," the voice said. "It will help you in your quest. Whenever you feel love in your heart, touch this pendant and say these words: I love you."

"What will happen then?" Erasto asked.

"You will see," the voice said mysteriously. "But remember love is an action. Love is a choice. Love is a commitment. To love someone is to care for them, to respect them, to support them, to trust them, to forgive them, to accept them, to grow with them."

He looked at each of them in turn. "Are you ready to take on this quest?" asked the voice.

Bayboo and Erasto nodded their heads. Tashi barked and wagged his tail.

"Very well then," said the voice of the Source of Kindness. "Go forth and spread love in the world. And remember, I'm always here if you need me."

It gave them a wink and a smile before it returned to its book.

They thanked the voice. They looked at each other with excitement and anticipation and left. They were ready to embark on their new quest. They were ready to spread love in the world.

Bayboo, Erasto, and their dog Tashi sought the wisdom from the Source of Kindness and learned that the secret to happiness is love. They were overjoyed by their discovery and decided to share it with the world. So, they set on a quest to spread love to everyone they'd meet.

Starting in their own village, they greeted their neighbors with smiles and hugs. They helped the elderly with their chores; played with the children and listened to the people's stories. They gave compliments, encouragement, and showed gratitude to everyone they encountered. They made everyone feel valued and appreciated and loved.

The villagers were amazed by the change in Bayboo, Erasto, and Tashi. They had never seen them so happy, kind, and loving before.

They wondered what had happened to them and what was their secret. They asked them why they were doing these things?

Bayboo, Erasto, and their dog Tashi told them all about their journey to see the Source of Kindness and the wisdom it had given them. They told them that love is the key to happiness, and they wanted to share it with everyone. They invited them to join their quest and spread love to others.

The villagers were touched by their words and inspired by their actions. They agreed to join their quest and spread love to others. They formed a group of love ambassadors and set out to other villages. They traveled from village to village spreading love wherever they went. They did acts of kindness, compassion, and generosity for the people they met.

They showed respect, empathy, and understanding for their differences.

They created bonds of friendship, trust, and harmony among the people.

They also taught them about the voice's secret to happiness and encouraged them to find love within themselves and others. They invited them to join their quest and share love with others. They invited them to join their quest and spread love to all. Soon, more people joined their quest to spread love. The love ambassadors grew in number and reached every corner of the world. They transformed the world with love.

Bayboo, Erasto, and Tashi were proud of their achievements and grateful for their experiences. They had fulfilled their quest and found happiness in love. They realized that love is not just a feeling, but a choice, an action, and a way of life.

One day they were enjoying a peaceful morning in the village. They had just finished their breakfast bars and milk and were planning to visit the nearby market. Bayboo wanted to buy seed for his garden and a new book about music. Erasto wanted to see the latest gadgets. And Tashi wanted to chase the pigeons. They were about to leave when they heard a loud noise outside. They rushed to the door and saw a crowd of people running in panic. They also saw a large airship with loudspeakers flying overhead dropping leaflets.

"Attention citizens of this land!" a voice boomed from the airship. "We are the Peacemakers, and we come to bring peace and harmony. We have a simple message for you: Join us or perish. We have the power and the technology to make this world a better place, but we need your cooperation. If you resist us, you will face our wrath. You have 24 hours to decide. Peace out."

The airship zoomed away, leaving behind a trail of smoke and fear. The villagers looked at each other in terror and confusion. What is this Peacemakers group? What did they want? How do we resist them, they wondered?

Bayboo, Erasto, and Tashi decided to act. They knew that this was not real peace, but tyranny. They had to stop them somehow. They packed their bags with some essentials and headed for the nearest town. They hoped to find some allies there, and more clues about the Peacemakers.

They boarded a bus that was headed to the next town. Along the way they saw more signs of the Peacemakers presence. They saw checkpoints, drones, cameras, and posters with slogans like "Peace is Power" and "Obey or Die." They also saw people wearing red uniforms with the symbol of a white dove on their chests. They were the Peacemakers agents, and they looked menacing.

Bayboo, Erasto, and Tashi got off and looked round. The town was bustling with activity, but also tense with fear. They saw more Peacemakers agents patrolling the streets and interrogating people.

They also saw some resistance fighters hiding in alleys and crouched on rooftops. They wore blue bandanas and carried weapons.

They quickly agreed to join the resistance. They were taken to a safehouse where they met some of the leaders of the movement. They introduced themselves and explained their situation.

"Welcome friends," one of the leaders said. "We are glad that you are here. We need all the help we can get. The Peacemakers are a powerful enemy, and they have been spreading their influence for months as a reaction to the love you spread. They claim to bring peace and love, but only bring oppression and violence. They have a secret base somewhere in the mountains where they keep a weapon that can destroy anything in its path. We have been trying to find and destroy it, but we have been unsuccessful, so far."

"Maybe we can help," Bayboo volunteered. "We have some skills and experiences that might be useful. We have been on many adventures before, and we have faced many dangers."

"Indeed," Erasto said. "And we have a brave and smart dog, too. Right, Tashi?"

Tashi barked, "Woof," and wagged his tail.

The leaders smiled and nodded.

"Very well," one of them said. "We are happy to have you on our side. We have a plan to infiltrate the Peacemakers' base and sabotage their weapon. But we need a small team of volunteers to do it."

The three of them looked at each other. Bayboo and Erasto said in unison, "We're ready."

Tashi panted his enthusiasm.

The leaders clasped their shoulders, "Excellent," one of them said. "Let's go over the details then."

They gathered around a map and began to discuss their strategy. The peace mission was about to begin.

III

Peace

Bayboo, Erasto, and Tashi ran as fast as they could dodging blasts that zapped the ground behind them. They had just escaped the Peacemakers prison where they had been interrogated and tortured for days after their capture while seeking to sabotage the secret weapon. They had managed to steal a key from one of the guards and unlock their cell, but they knew they were not yet safe. The Peacemakers were relentless in their pursuit of anyone who threatened their rule.

"Where are we going, Bayboo," Erasto asked, panting.

"We need to find the resistance," Bayboo said. "They're the ones who can help us fight back."

"But how can we find them," Erasto asked. "We don't even know where they are."

"Woof," Tashi barked in agreement.

Bayboo looked around, trying to spot a sign of hope. They were in the deserted part of the town, where the buildings were crumbling, and the streets were littered with trash.

The Peacemakers had destroyed most of the infrastructure and resources, leaving people in poverty and despair. Bayboo remembered how life was before the Peacemakers came. How they used to laugh and play with their friends in the village. How they enjoyed the fresh air and the green fields. How they were filled with love and kindness for each other. Now, everything was gone. Everything except Tashi, their loyal dog, who had found them through their ordeal.

"Erasto, look," Bayboo said pointing to the graffiti on a wall. It was the symbol of a fist holding a rose, surrounded by the words, "Peace is possible." It was the mark of the resistance, and a sign that they were still fighting against the Peacemakers. Bayboo was encouraged and guessed that they might be near. "They said they had a hidden base somewhere in the mountains, where they planned their attacks, and trained their soldiers." Although they had met many of their leaders, they had never met the mysterious leader who went by the name of "The Rose."

"Maybe they are nearby," Bayboo said. "Maybe we can find them, and they can help us."

"Or maybe it's a trap," Erasto said. "How do we know this isn't the work of the Peacemakers to lure us into their trap?"

"We don't," Bayboo said. "But we must take the chance. They're our only hope."

They decided to follow the graffiti, hoping it would lead them to resistance. They walked for hours avoiding the main roads and surveillance cameras. They saw more signs of the resistance along the way, such as posters, stickers, and flyers. They also saw more signs of the Peacemakers' oppression, such as check points, patrols, and propaganda.

They saw people who looked scared, hungry, and hopeless. They saw people who looked angry, defiant, and rebellious, too. They saw people who looked like them.

They finally reached the outskirts of the town, where the buildings gave way to the hills. They climbed a steep slope, following a trail that had been marked by the resistance symbol. They found a cave entrance that was hidden by some bushes. They pushed them aside and entered the cave. Hoping to find members of the resistance inside, they were greeted by a blast of chilly air and a loud bark, as Tashi had run ahead and found something in the cave. They heard a voice say, "Who are you and what are you doing here?"

They followed Tashi and saw a man standing in front of them. He was wearing a leather jacket, a blue bandana, and a pair of sunglasses. He had a gun in his hand and a knife in his belt. He looked tough and dangerous.

"We're looking for the resistance," Bayboo said. We worked with them in another town to defeat the Peacemakers. Unfortunately, we were captured, but we escaped. Are you part of the resistance?"

The man looked at them suspiciously. "Maybe I am, maybe I'm not," he said. "Why should I trust you?"

"Because we're on your side," Erasto said. "We hate the Peacemakers as much as you. They took everything from us. They killed family and friends. They tortured us and tried to break us, but we escaped. We want to join you. We want to fight back."

The man lowered his gun slightly. "How do I know you're not lying? How do I know you're not spies sent by the Peacemakers?"

"You don't," Bayboo said. "But we have nothing to lose. We have nowhere else to go. We have no one else to trust. Please, help us."

The man looked at them for a long time. He looked at their faces, their clothes, their wounds. He looked at Tashi who wagged his tail and licked his hand. He looked at the graffiti on the wall, the symbol of resistance. He looked at his own heart, the symbol of his faith.

He finally said, "All right, I'll help you, but you must prove yourselves. You must pass a test."

"What kind of test?" Bayboo asked.

The man smiled and said, "Follow me and you'll see."

He led them into the cave, where they saw a group of people waiting for them. They wore similar outfits to the man, and they carried various weapons and gadgets. They looked like a ragtag army, ready for war.

"These are my comrades, the resistance fighters," the man said.

"We are the ones who follow the Rose." He pointed to a large screen on a wall, where a video was playing. It showed a woman wearing a hooded cloak, holding a rose in her hand. She wore a mask covering her face, hiding her identity. She had a voice that was calm, confident, inspiring, and commanding.

"Greetings, my fellow rebels," she said. "I am the leader of the resistance. I have a message for you. The time has come to strike. The time has come to end the Peacemakers tyranny. The time has come to restore peace to the world. We have a plan, a plan that will change everything. We have a target, a target that will make them pay. We have a weapon, a weapon that will give us the edge. We have a hope, a hope that will keep us alive. We have each other, and we have the rose."

"The rose is our symbol, our sign, our secret. The rose is our power, our weapon, our hope. The rose is the key to peace. And we are the ones who will use it. We are the ones who will make it happen. We are the ones who will make history. We are the rose, and we are ready. Are you?"

The video ended and the screen went blank. The man turned to Bayboo and Erasto and said, "That was the Rose. She is our leader. She is our hero. She is our hope. She has a plan, a plan that will put an end to the Peacemakers. She has a weapon. A weapon that will give us the edge. She has a secret that only we know. And she has a test. A test that only you can take. If you want to join us, if you want to be a part of the resistance, if you want to be a part of the rose, you must pass the test. You must find the rose. The rose is hidden somewhere in this cave. The rose is the key to peace. You must find it. You have 10 minutes. Go!"

He pushed a button and a timer started counting down. Bayboo and Erasto looked at each other confused and concerned. They didn't know what to do. They didn't know where to go. They didn't know what the rose was. They only knew they had to find it. They had to find it, or they would fail. They had to find it, or they would lose their chance to fight for peace. They had to find it, or they would die.

They ran into the cave, searching for the rose. They looked everywhere, under rocks, behind stalagmites, inside crevices. They found nothing. They grew more desperate, more frantic, more hopeless. They were running out of time, out of options, out of luck. They were running out of hope.

They reached the end of the cave, where they saw a dead end. They saw a stone wall blocking their way. They saw a sign that said, the rose is not here. The rose is not anywhere. The rose is not what you think. The rose is not what you seek. The rose is not a flower. The rose is not a key. The rose is not a secret. The rose is not a thing. The rose is a person. The rose is you.

The man tells them that they are the ones chosen to fight against the Peacekeepers. Their mission is to infiltrate the Peacemakers headquarters and steal the secret weapon.

"But Bayboo, we have tried and failed before," Erasto said.

"Yes, but we never give up," Bayboo said and smiled his encouragement to his grandson, and their dog, Tashi.

The man gave them a map and a clue to find the secret weapon, and warned them they will face many dangers, and enemies along the way.

Bayboo, Erasto, and Tashi accept the challenge and embark on the perilous quest. Along the way they use their skills, courage, and teamwork to overcome obstacles, traps, drones, and cyborgs.

They finally reached the Peacemakers headquarters and located the secret weapon, which turned out to be the portable laser cannon the Peacemakers fired at them during their escape. It vaporizes anything in its path. Working quickly and quietly, they dismantle the laser cannon and escape with it, but not before being spotted by the Peacemakers' leader, who recognizes them as the escaped prisoners, and vows to hunt them down.

They return to the cave and present the weapon to the resistance, who congratulate and welcome them as allies. They are praised for proving themselves worthy of the task.

The man then turns to the dark screen and the Rose appears. The Rose also praises them. "Because of your success you are worthy of knowing our true purpose."

Together they say, "To unite the world under the banner of love and overthrow the Peacemakers, we earn our peace back."

The Rose asks, "Bayboo, Erasto, and Tashi, will you join the resistance and lead the final assault on the Peacemakers stronghold using the power of the rose to bring peace to the world?"

Bayboo, Erasto, and Tashi agree and prepare for the ultimate battle. They rallied the people and inspired them with Rose's message of love.

Meanwhile, they devised a plan to use the laser cannon to breach the Peacemakers defenses and use the Rose to confront the Peacemaker leader and persuade him to surrender or face the consequences.

The battle begins and the resistance launches a massive attack on the stronghold. Bayboo, Erasto, and Tashi lead the charge using the laser cannon to blast a hole in the wall. They enter the stronghold and fight their way to the leader's chamber, where they engage him and his elite guards.

The leader says, "Your rose is useless against me, and I will crush you and your pathetic resistance like bugs," he taunts. "Attack them," he yells.

But Bayboo, Erasto, and Tashi use Rose's power to fend them off to reach the leader.

They corner the leader and try to reason with him, telling him the war is over and to accept Rose's offer of peace and love. "The Rose can heal your wounds and your heart. There's still time to redeem yourself and choose peace," Bayboo said.

The leader refuses and tries to kill them with his own weapon, a plasma sword. He swings the sword at them, but the Rose blocks his attack and emits a bright light that blinds him and his guards.

The Rose then speaks to the leader and tells him he has one last chance to choose love over hate. And peace over war, or else he will face the wrath of the Rose.

The leader is stunned and confused by Rose's voice and power of love. A sensation fills his chest. It is as if his heart is melting. He drops his sword and falls to his knees. He looks at the Rose and sees visions of his past, when he was a young and innocent boy who loved animals and nature. He also sees a vision of his future, when he could be a happy and peaceful man who loves and is loved by others. In that moment he realizes that he is wasting his life on war and violence, and this is a chance for him to change and start anew.

The leader looks at them and sees them as friends, not enemies. A surge of tears and emotion fills his eyes. He reaches out his hand and says, "I'm sorry. Please forgive me. I choose peace and love."

They tell him that Rose also forgives him and that it will help him heal and start a new life.

The Rose also smiles and tells him that it is proud of him and welcomes him as a friend. The Rose tells them that they have completed the mission and brought peace back into the world.

The Rose emits a powerful wave of light that spreads throughout the world, healing the wounds of the war and restoring the balance of nature. The people of the world feel Rose's presence and message of love. They rejoice and celebrate the end of the war and the dawn of a new era of peace and harmony.

Bayboo, Erasto, Tashi, and the leader join the people and share their joy and gratitude. They thank Rose for its guidance and its gift. The Rose thanks them for their courage and their love. It calls them true heroes and promises it will always be with them in their hearts.

The Rose fades away, leaving behind a beautiful fragrant flower that symbolizes its legacy. They pick up the flower and take turns holding it close to their chests. They smile at each other, knowing they have found loyal friends and their true love. Looking at the sky they see a rainbow that reflects the world's future. They are happy and fulfilled, then Erasto says, "Bayboo, wouldn't it be fitting to go on a quest for goodness?"

IV

Goodness

The quest for goodness got off to an admirable start. Bayboo, Erasto, and Tashi had been traveling for days, following the map that the Rose had left for them. They were looking for the Temple of Goodness where they hoped to find the answers to their questions about goodness. They had faced more hardship and danger than expected, but they never gave up hope.

One day, they reached a vast desert, where the sun was scorching, and the sand was burning. They had only a little water left, and they knew they needed to find shelter soon. They saw a mirage of an oasis in the distance, but they were unsure if it was real. They decided to take the chance and follow it.

As they came closer, Bayboo said, "Look, Erasto, it is real."

"Yes, Bayboo, the water is a clear pool of blue, and the palm trees and the flowers are so beautiful and fragrant," Erasto said.

"Woof, woof," Tashi barked in agreement and wagged his tail as he ran to the water.

They also spotted a small hut, made of mud and straw. They ran toward the oasis, eager to quench their thirst and rest their weary bodies.

They splashed some water on their faces. Tashi jumped in and swam happily. Bayboo and Erasto smiled, feeling relieved and grateful. Then they noticed a sign next to the hut, which read: "Welcome to the Oasis of Goodness. I am the guardian of this place. Please feel free to use the hut and the pool, but do not disturb the peace. If you need anything, just ring the bell and I will come to help you. May you find what you are looking for."

Bayboo and Erasto were curious about the Guardian, but they decided to respect his wishes and not disturb him. Inside the hut they found food and blankets. They filled themselves eating fruit and bread, then they laid down on the mats. They fell asleep feeling full, safe, and comfortable.

The next morning, they woke up to the sound of the bell ringing in their ears. They got up, and went outside, wondering who had rung it. They saw a man standing by the pool, holding a staff. He had a long beard, and he wore a turban, and a white robe.

He looked at them with a kind smile and said, "Hello Travelers, I am the Guardian of this oasis. I hope you had a good night's rest."

They nodded their heads.

"Good. I rang the bell to invite you to join me for breakfast. Please, come in and sit with me."

Bayboo and Erasto were surprised and delighted by the Guardian's hospitality. They thanked him and followed him to a table where he had prepared some tea and fruit. They sat down and introduced themselves, and then told him about their quest.

The Guardian listened attentively, nodding, and smiling. He said, "I see. You are looking for the Temple of Goodness, where you hope to find out about goodness. This is a noble and worthy quest, indeed. I admire your courage and your determination. You have come a long way, and you have faced many challenges. You are amazingly close to your destination, but you have one more test to pass."

Bayboo and Erasto looked at him in anticipation, as Tashi cocked his head to the side. The curiosity was overwhelming, so they asked, "What test? What do we have to do?"

"The test of goodness," the Guardian said. "You see, this is not only a place for rest and refreshment. It is also a place of learning and enlightenment. Here, you can find the goodness you need to enter the Temple of Goodness. But goodness is not something you can get easily. You must earn it by proving that you are worthy of it. You must show that you have a good heart, a good mind, and a good soul."

Bayboo and Erasto wondered what he meant given all that they had learned. Erasto asked, "How can we show that we have those qualities, sir?"

The Guardian said, "By answering three questions. Each question will challenge a different aspect of your goodness. If you want to enter the Temple of Goodness, you must answer each question correctly. If you answer them correctly, you will prove that you are good, and I will let you pass. But if you answer them wrong, you will show that you are not good, and I will send you back. Do you accept the challenge?" the Guardian asked.

They looked at each other and nodded, as Tashi's tongue slid out of the side of his mouth. They agreed to take the challenge.

"Very well, then, the gift of goodness is the ultimate virtue, encompassing, love, joy, peace, patience, kindness, gentleness, faith, and self-control," the Guardian said.

"The first challenge is for your heart. You must each choose one person from your past who has hurt you or wronged you and forgive them sincerely with all your heart. You must ask for their forgiveness for any harm you may have caused them. Only then will you be able to open the door to the next challenge," the Guardian said.

His voice fell silent, and the three of them looked at each other: the grandfather, grandson, and their dog. Each thought of someone who had wronged or hurt them in the past.

Bayboo thought of his father, who had abandoned him and his mother when he was a child. Erasto thought of his brother, who had betrayed him and stole his inheritance. Tashi thought of the trainer who had abused and discouraged him when he was a pup. Each of them felt a surge of anger, resentment, and pain.

They realized that this was not an easy challenge. It required them to let go of their grudges and bitterness, and to embrace forgiveness, and reconciliation. They wondered if they could do it. They wondered if they wanted to do it.

They decided to try. They closed their eyes and imagined the person they had chosen. They spoke to them in their minds, expressing their feelings and their wishes. They offered their forgiveness and asked for theirs. Suddenly, they felt a weight lift from their chests, and a warmth filled their hearts. They opened their eyes and saw that the door to the next challenge had opened.

They smiled at each other and entered the door.

"The second challenge is for the soul," the Guardian said, as they entered a room that was filled with mirrors.

"You must look into the mirror and see yourself as you truly are. You must accept your strengths and weaknesses, your virtues and your flaws, your successes, and your failures. You must also see your potential and your purpose, your gifts and your passions, your values, and your goals. Only then will you be able to open the door to your next challenge," the Guardian said.

The Guardian fell silent, as the three looked into the mirrors. They each saw their own reflection, but also something more. They saw their past, present, and their future. They saw their joys, their sorrows, and their hopes. They saw their achievements, their mistakes, and their lessons. The saw their talents, their limitations, and their opportunities. They saw themselves. They realized this was not an easy challenge, as well. It required them to face their reality and possibility, to embrace their identity and destiny. They wondered if they could do it. They wondered if they wanted to do it.

They decided to try. They looked into the mirrors and saw themselves as they were. They spoke to themselves in their minds, expressing their gratitude and aspirations. They accepted and affirmed themselves. They felt a goodness shine from their souls, and a peace filled their minds. They opened their eyes and saw that the door to the next challenge had opened.

They smiled at each other and walked through the door.

"The third challenge is for the mind," said the Guardian as they entered a room that was filled with books. "Each of you must choose one of these books from this library and read it. You must understand the meaning, its message, its wisdom, its facts, and opinions. You must also apply its knowledge and insights to your own life and to the world around you. Only then will you be able to open the door to the Temple of Goodness," the Guardian said.

He fell silent, and the three of them looked at the books. They each saw thousands of books, covering every topic and every genre imaginable.

They saw books on history, science, philosophy, religion, literature, art, and more. They saw books that were ancient, and books that were modern, books that were famous and books that were obscure, books that were simple and books that were complex. They saw books.

They realized that this challenge was not any easier than the others. It required them to choose wisely and read carefully, to comprehend deeply and think critically, to learn broadly and apply. They wondered if they could do it. They wondered if they wanted to do it.

They decided to try. They each picked a book that appealed to them and started to read it. Tashi grabbed a book called, "How to be Man's Best Friend" between his teeth and laid it under his head. They immersed themselves in the words and ideas, the arguments and the evidence, the stories, and the characters. They questioned, analyzed, evaluated, and synthesized. They learned, understood, appreciated, and applied. They felt a power grow in their minds, and a curiosity fill their spirits. They finished reading and saw that the door to the Temple of Goodness had opened.

They smiled at each other and walked through the door. They entered a room that was filled with Goodness.

The Guardian spoke again. "Congratulations, seekers of goodness. You have passed the three challenges. You have shown goodness of heart, soul, and mind. You are now ready to receive the gift of goodness. The gift of goodness is not something that can be given or taken away. It is something that can only be cultivated and practiced. It is something that can only be found in yourselves and shared with others. It is something that can only be lived and experienced. The gift of goodness is not a destination, but a journey. A journey that never ends, but always begins; a journey that you have already started and will continue to follow. A journey that will bring you joy, peace, and fulfillment. A journey that will make you a blessing to the world. A journey that will make you good."

The Guardian fell silent, and the three of them looked at each other.

Each felt a warmth in their hearts, a goodness in their souls, and a power in their minds. Each felt joy, peace, and fulfillment. Each of them felt goodness within them.

They realized that this was the Gift of Goodness. They realized that they always had it, and always would. They realized that they had found it, and always could. They realized that they had received it, and always should.

They thanked the Guardian. They celebrated their achievement and their friendship. They decided to continue their quest. They decided to live their goodness and share it with others. They smiled at each other, then shared a group hug, with Tashi in the middle.

V

Gentleness

Bayboo, Erasto, and their dog, Tashi, finally completed the quest for goodness, after facing many challenges and dangers along the way. They had learned the values of kindness, honesty, compassion, and courage, and they felt a sense of peace and joy in their hearts. But their journey was not over yet. They still had another quest to fulfill: the quest for gentleness. They had to find the hidden Sanctuary of the Gentle Spirit, where they would receive blessings and wisdom. To reach the sanctuary, they had to cross the gulf of rough waters, a vast and turbulent sea that was home to many mysterious creatures and secrets. They knew it would not be easy, but they knew they had each other, and that would be enough to keep them going.

The trio boarded a small boat that belonged to a friendly fisher, who agreed to take them across the gulf. He warned them that the sea was unpredictable and full of surprises, and that they should be prepared for anything. He also told them that the Sanctuary of the Gentle Spirit was hidden on a small island surrounded by thick fog that only lifted for those who had a pure and gentle heart. He said he had never seen the island himself, but that he had heard stories from sailors who had briefly glimpsed it. "Good luck Bayboo, Erasto, and Tashi," he said, and set sail.

As they sailed, they enjoyed the breeze, and Bayboo said, "Erasto, what a gentle breeze. Look at the beautiful waves."

"Bayboo, look at those dolphins jumping up out of the water," Erasto marveled.

"Woof, woof," Tashi barked, when he saw whales spouting water in the distance, as colorful fish swam under the boat.

They also saw some strange and wonderful things, such as a giant turtle with a forest on its back, a flying fish with wings, and a mermaid singing a beautiful song. They felt a sense of wonder and gratitude for the beauty of nature, and they thanked the fisher for his kindness and generosity.

Suddenly the boat was rocked by a huge wave, and they heard a loud roar from behind. They turned around and saw a massive sea dragon with green and gold scales, and eyes of fire. It looked angry and fierce, as it headed straight towards them. The fisher panicked and tried to steer the boat away, but it was too late. The sea dragon opened his mouth and swallowed the boat whole, along with the fisher, Bayboo, Erasto, and Tashi. They found themselves in the dark belly of the beast, surrounded by bones, and debris.

"Bayboo, what do we do?" Erasto asked terrified.

Bayboo was confused and wondered if this was the end of their quest.

"Let us join hands and pray for a miracle," Bayboo said.

Then they heard a voice in their minds, calm and gentle, say, "Do not be afraid, my children. You are safe and welcome here. I am the Protector of the sanctuary and I have brought you here to test your hearts. If you pass the test, you will see the island and receive the blessing and wisdom of gentleness. If you fail, you will be returned to the sea, and you will have to try again. Are you ready for your test," the Protector asked?

Then they saw a glimpse of the voice in their minds and were shocked and amazed that it was the sea dragon. They realized that it was not a monster, but the Protector of the Sanctuary of the Gentle Spirit. They felt a surge of hope and curiosity, and gratefulness that their prayer had been answered, and decided to accept the test.

They replied to the voice in their minds as one, "Yes, we ready for the test."

"We have come far to complete our quest for gentleness, and we are willing to accept the challenge," Bayboo said. "Please, tell us what we have to do?"

The voice of the sea dragon said, "Very well, my children, the test is simple, but not easy.

"The sea dragon is a mighty beast that rules the oceans, but he has a secret in his heart, that he wishes to keep. He longs for a companion who can share his lonely fate, but he fears none can match his strength or endure his hate. So, I devised a test of gentleness to find one who is worthy," he sang.

Bayboo, Erasto, and Tashi each had a different skill, but shared a common bond and a spirit of goodwill and listened intently. The test was simple, but not easy. They had to touch his scales without causing him any pain or harm or making him wail.

Bayboo tried to use his speed and darted around the Protector, but he scratched the sea dragon's skin by mistake, and angered the beast.

Erasto tried to use his strength and pushed against the scales. But he bruised the dragon's flesh with force and made him flail.

Tashi tried to use his wisdom and studied the sea dragon's form. He noticed a spot behind his ear that looked soft and warm. He approached him gently and whispered in his ear. He said, "I am not afraid." And to show his courage, he gently stroked his scales with care.

The Protector felt a surge of pure joy and calmness in his chest. He realized that Tashi had passed his test of gentleness and asked him to stay. He offered his friendship, and a regal place in his realm.

Tashi smiled, and barked, "Woof, woof," ("Okay for a while"). He knew that he had found a friend indeed by the sea dragon's test, and that he was needed.

During his time with the Protector, Tashi learned that gentleness is a strength of character that involves being calm, soft, supportive, and respectful in the face of challenges of adversity. And that's the way they lived their lives until it was time for him to return to Bayboo and Erasto.

VI

Joy

Bayboo, Erasto, and their dog, Tashi were bored. They had nothing to do on a rainy Saturday afternoon. They played chess, watched their favorite shows, and read all their books. They wanted to do something fun, something exciting, something that would make them joyful.

They decided to go on a quest for joy. They pulled on their raincoats and boots, grabbed their umbrellas, and headed outside. They walked around their neighborhood looking for signs of joy. They saw a rainbow in the sky, found a puddle to splash in, a flower to smell, returned a baby bird to its nest, and spotted a friend to wave at. They felt a little bit of joy in these things, but they wanted more.

They kept walking until they reached the park. There, they saw a big sign that said, "Joy Festival." They were curious and decided to check it out. They entered the park and saw lots of people having fun. There were games, rides, music, and laughter. They played ring toss, rode the Ferris Wheel, ate cotton candy, danced to the beat, and laughed with the clowns. They felt joy in doing each of these things, but they wanted more.

They kept exploring until they reached the center of the park. There they saw a huge tent that said, "The Joy of Giving."

Intrigued, they decided to go there and entered the tent. Inside, they saw a lot of people giving and receiving gifts. There were toys, books, clothes, and money. They saw smiles, tears, hugs, and gratitude. They felt the joy surge in their hearts. They realized that this was what they were looking for. They decided to join in the joy of giving.

"Erasto," Bayboo said. "Look around and see what we can give."

"Yes, Bayboo," Erasto said. "I see a boy over there that I can give my raincoat to."

"That girl over there, Erasto. She is wet and shivering. I will give my umbrella to her," Bayboo said.

"Look, Bayboo," Erasto said. "Tashi gave his bone to that hungry dog."

They felt a warm glow in their chests, as the boy, the girl, and the dog smiled and thanked them. The trio felt a real connection. They felt the joy of giving.

They looked around and saw what they could receive. "Thank you," Bayboo said to a man, "for these wonderful balloons."

The man bowed and was cheerful and kind.

Erasto received a comic book from a wise and witty woman wearing galoshes.

Tashi barked, "Woof," as he caught a ball from a playful and friendly kid. A cool breeze caressed their faces. They saw the man, the woman, and the kid smile and wave at them. They felt a strong bond with them. They felt the joy of receiving.

When they left the tent, the rain had stopped, and the sun was shining. And they felt joy in their souls. They had found the joy they were looking for.

Bayboo, Erasto, and Tashi decided to spread the joy they had found at the joy festival. They wanted to make other people joyful. They thought of diverse ways to do it. They decided to use their gifts, talents, and passions to share with others.

Bayboo loved art. He decided to use his balloons to make balloon animals for the kids. He twisted and turned the different colored balloons into many shapes. He made dogs, cats, monkeys, giraffes, and unicorns, then gave them to the kids he passed on the street. He felt the joy of receiving when he saw their eyes light up with awe, and their mouths curve into smiles.

Erasto loved to read. He decided to use his comic book to read stories to seniors. He read aloud to the seniors he visited at the nursing home. He added his own jokes from his imaginative sense of humor, to make it more fun. He brought them to laughter, as they remembered their own youth. He laughed too, as he saw their wrinkles soften and their spirits lift. He felt joy just by reading.

Tashi loved to play. He decided to use his ball to play with other dogs. He ran and chased the ball with the dogs he encountered at the park. He shared his ball with them, and everybody had a turn. They wagged their tails and barked with delight. He saw their ears perk up and their energy surge. He felt joy playing with others.

After a long day of spreading joy, they returned home. They were tired but were full of joy. They had made other people joyful, just like they were. They had used their gifts, talents, and passions to share joy with others. The joy of spreading joy filled their spirits.

Bayboo, Erasto, and Tashi wanted to spread more joy the next day. They put their heads together and thought of new ways to do that. "I know," Bayboo said. "This time we will use skills, hobbies, and interests to share joy with others.

"Yes," Erasto said.

"Woof," Tashi barked.

Bayboo loved music. "I've decided to use my guitar and play songs for others," he said. He strummed and sang songs he knew and had learned when he was a small boy. He sang happy songs, sad songs, funny songs, and love songs. He sang to strangers he met at the bus stop, the coffee shop, the library, and the mall. He watched their ears perk up, and their lips sing along. They felt the joy of music.

Erasto loved to bake. "I'll use my oven to bake cookies for our neighbors," he said. He mixed and baked cookies from the recipes he had learned. He baked chocolate chip cookies, oatmeal cookies, peanut butter cookies, and snickerdoodles. He liked to see their noses twitch, and their mouths water when they smelled his cookies. They felt the joy of his baking.

Tashi loved to explore. He decided to use his nose to sniff out treasures for others. He found a ring, a watch, a key, and a coin. He returned them to their owners, and cocked his head to the side when he saw their eyes widen and clasp their hands to their faces. They felt the joy of his explorations.

They returned home after another day of spreading joy. They were tired, but joyful they had made more people joyful, just like they were. They had used their skills, hobbies, and interests to share joy with others. They felt the joy of spreading joy, but they had learned something else, too.

Bayboo, Erasto and Tashi learned that true joy comes from within.

They learned that they didn't need to depend on external things or people to bring them joy. They discovered that they had everything they needed inside themselves. It gave them a sense of peace, freedom, and fulfillment.

Bayboo was joyful. He understood that he didn't have to worry about what others thought of him or what he lacked. He accepted himself and his life as they were. He was content with what he had and grateful for what he got. He was calm and serene.

"Bayboo, I feel free," Erasto said. "I realize that I don't have to seek what others offered or what I wanted. I enjoyed myself and my friends as they are." He was loyal to what he loved and generous in what he shared. He was joyous.

They felt joyous inside. They learned they could create their own joy, no matter what. They decided to live joyfully, and every day experience the joy of living.

VII

Patience

"Hey Bayboo, do you know where I can find more patience," Erasto asked, as he sighed anxiously.

"Patience? Why do you need more patience?" Bayboo asked.

"Because I want to be calmer and more peaceful," Erasto said.

"Well, patience is not something that you can find," Bayboo said. "It is something you have to cultivate."

"Cultivate?" Erasto said.

Erasto was a curious and restless boy who always wanted to learn new things and explore unfamiliar places. He admired the ones in the Temple of Goodness and wanted to be patient, like them. "I wonder how they achieved such patience?" Erasto asked his grandfather, Bayboo. "You're wise, will you teach me to have more patience, please?"

"Yes Erasto, I will teach you that patience requires being mindful, attentive, and compassionate in every moment. Patience accepts things as they are without judgment or resistance," he said. "Patience requires letting go of expectations and attachments, and being open to whatever happens."

Erasto was intrigued by Bayboo's words. "How can I cultivate patience?" he asked.

Bayboo said the first step was to breath deeply and relax his body, then focus his attention on his breath, and nothing else. He said that if any thoughts or feelings arose, he should just observe and stay in the present moment.

Erasto agreed to try and followed his grandfather's instructions. He took a deep breath, and relaxed his body, then focused his attention on his breath, and nothing else. He observed the thoughts and feelings that arose, and let them go without reacting to them, or following them. He returned to his breath and stayed in the present moment. He felt a sense of calmness and clarity, and he enjoyed the sensation. Thank you, Bayboo for your guidance, but how long do I have to practice patience?" he asked.

Bayboo smiled and said, "There is no fixed time for practicing patience. For some people it takes a lifetime. For others it just takes a moment. The important thing is to keep trying, and to never give up. Patience is a skill that improves with practice, and it will bring you many benefits, such as happiness, peace, and wisdom," Bayboo said.

Erasto nodded, and said, "I understand. I'm willing to listen and learn, Bayboo. What else must I do to cultivate patience?" Erasto asked.

Bayboo told him the next step was to apply patience to his daily life, and to every situation he encountered. "Erasto, you must be mindful, attentive, and compassionate in every interaction and activity. Learn to accept things as they are without judging or resisting them. And let go of your expectations and attachments, and be open to whatever happens," Bayboo said.

"Bayboo, give me an example of how I can do that," Erasto said.

"We can start with something simple, like playing with Tashi. Tashi is a friendly and playful dog. He always has a smile, wags his tail, and licks our hands and faces. Tashi is also a good teacher because he is always present in the moment and always happy," Bayboo said.

Erasto agreed that Tashi was a good boy, and said, "I love playing with him. But Bayboo, how can I practice patience while playing with Tashi?"

Bayboo told him that he could practice patience by being mindful of Tashi's feelings and needs. And being attentive to his actions and reactions. He said that he could practice patience by being compassionate to Tashi, and by responding to him with kindness and respect. He said that he could practice patience by accepting Tashi as he is without judging or resisting him, and by letting go of expectations and attachments, by being open to whatever happens.

Erasto said, "I'll try that," and went to play with Tashi. He petted Tashi, and said, "Hello."

"Woof, woof," Tashi barked as he licked his hand, and wagged his tail.

Erasto was mindful of Tashi's feelings and needs, and he was attentive to his actions and reactions. He was compassionate with Tashi and responded with kindness and respect. He accepted Tashi as he was without judging or resisting him. He let go of his expectations and attachments and was open to whatever happened.

"Woof, woof," Tashi was happy and grateful, and showed his affection to Erasto.

Erasto felt a sense of joy and connection. "Thank you, Tashi, for your friendship," he said. He realized he was practicing patience, and that made him feel good. He also realized Tashi was practicing patience, and that it made him feel good, too.

When he went back to his grandfather, he told him what he had experienced. "I learned a lot from playing with Tashi," Erasto said. I'd like to continue practicing patience and apply it to other aspects of my life."

Bayboo was proud and happy for his grandson and praised him for his progress. "You have done a great job and are a good student," he said.

"Thank you for helping me practice patience, Bayboo," Erasto said.

"I have learned from you, too," Bayboo said. He also said that he was grateful for his curiosity and enthusiasm. They hugged, then thanked Tashi, too.

"You are a loving dog and will always be a part of our family. And now that all of us are practicing patience, it makes us happier and wiser," Erasto said.

They smiled and laughed and enjoyed the moment. They shared a sense of harmony and gratitude, as they realized they had found patience, not by looking for it, but cultivating it.

After playing, Bayboo, Erasto, and Tashi decided to go for a walk in the nearby park. They wanted to enjoy the fresh air, and practice patience in a different setting.

They pulled on their shoes and jackets, leashed Tashi, and left the house walking towards the park. The park was near their home. They greeted friends and neighbors along the way and arrived in no time. They smiled at the strangers they encountered, responding to them with kindness and respect. They accepted things like they were without judging or resisting them. They let go of their expectations and attachments and were open to whatever happened.

When they entered the park, they saw that it was crowded with people and animals. There were children playing, adults chatting, dogs barking, birds singing, and squirrels running. There were flowers blooming, trees swaying, leaves falling, and water flowing. There was sound, color, and movement everywhere. It was a lively and beautiful scene, but also a challenging one for practicing patience.

Bayboo, Erasto and Tashi looked for a place to sit and relax. They found a bench near a pond and sat down. They breathed deeply, and relaxed their bodies, as they focused on their breath, and nothing else. They tried to ignore the noise and distractions around them, and to stay in the present moment.

They did this for a while and felt a sense of calmness and clarity. They thanked each other for their company and asked how each other felt. Feeling good, they continued to enjoy the park.

They decided to continue their walk further and explore the park. Leaving the bench, they walked along a path. They admired the beauty and diversity of the park and appreciated the gift of nature. They were mindful of their steps, and attentive to their senses. They were compassionate to the plants and animals and responded to them with care and curiosity. They accepted things as they were without judging or resisting them, and let go of their expectations and attachments, and were open to whatever happened.

They walked for a while and stumbled upon various situations that tested their patience. They met a rude and angry man, who yelled at them for no reason. They met a lost and scared child, who cried for their parents. They met a hungry homeless man, who asked them for food. They met a sick and injured dog, who limped and whimpered. They met a happy and friendly girl, who invited them to play.

They handled each situation with patience and did their best to comfort and help those in need, and to forgive those who harmed them. They accepted those who shared their joy and included them in their fun. And learned from each experience and grew in patience.

They returned to the bench and sat down again. They breathed deep and relaxed their bodies, and focused on their breath, and nothing else. They reflected on their walk and shared their thoughts and feelings.

Bayboo said, "I learned a lot from the park, Erasto."

"Yes, Bayboo," Erasto said. "I feel calmer and more peaceful."

"Woof, woof, woof," Tashi barked.

"Let's keep practicing patience, and apply it to all aspects of our lives," Erasto said.

Bayboo hugged his grandson and praised him for his progress. "You have done an excellent job, Erasto, and you are such a good student," Bayboo said. "But I learned from you, too. I an grateful for your curiosity and enthusiasm."

"Thank you, Bayboo for being a loving grandfather who finds delight in teaching."

"Woof," Tashi barked, and leaned onto Bayboo's legs to show his affection.

"Tashi, we love you, too, and you are a vital part of our family," he said. They all were practicing patience, and it made them happier and wiser.

They smiled, laughed, and enjoyed the moment. They shared a sense of harmony and gratitude, as they realized that they had found patience by not looking for it, but by cultivating it.

VIII

Faith

Bayboo, Erasto, and Tashi had been travelling for three days following the clues left by the Source of Kindness, who had mysteriously disappeared while searching for a lost manuscript of faith. The manuscript was said to contain ancient secrets about the origins of faith and the nature of God. The Source had dedicated its life to studying the history of spirituality and believed that the manuscript was hidden somewhere in a city a long way from the village, in a secret vault guarded by a puzzle box.

The trio arrived in the city, where they rented a small apartment near the city library. They spent hours browsing through the vast collection of books, maps, and documents, looking for hints or references for the manuscript. They also visited several historic sites like City Abbey, City Towers, and the Great Cathedral, hoping to find some clues in the architecture or the art.

But so far, they had found nothing. No matter how hard they searched they could not find any trace of the Source, the manuscript, or the puzzle box. They were starting to lose hope, and wondered if they were on the wrong track.

"Bayboo, maybe we should try a different approach," Erasto suggested, as they returned to their apartment after another fruitless day. "Maybe we should look for people who know something about the manuscript instead of just places."

"Like whom," Bayboo asked, feeling tired and frustrated.

"I don't know, some scholars, historians, or experts of medieval manuscripts. Someone who works at the library, or a professor at a university. Someone who belongs to a secret society, or a cult, or a religious order. Someone who has a connection to the Source of Kindness, or to the manuscript itself."

"That sounds like a lot of someone's," Bayboo said. "How are we going to find these people? And how do we know they will tell us the truth, or not try to stop us, or take the manuscript for themselves?"

"We have to be careful, of course," Erasto said.

"Woof," barked Tashi.

"But we can't just keep looking at buildings and books," Erasto said. "We need to talk to people, to hear their stories, to see their perspectives. They can help us understand what the manuscript is and why it's so important."

Bayboo nodded, feeling a sense of pride in Erasto's growth and spark of curiosity. He had always loved listening to stories, especially stories about faith and spirituality. He wondered what kind of stories these people would tell, and what kind of secrets they would reveal.

"Okay, let's do it. Let's find some people who know something about the manuscript. But where to start?" Bayboo wondered.

Erasto smiled and pulled out his laptop. He opened a web browser and typed in a search query: a quest for faith story.

"Let's see what the internet has to say," he said, and clicked the first result.

"Faith begins when we trust and obey God," Erasto read from the screen.

"Faith is shown when we truly believe that God always wants what's best for us," Bayboo read, "trusting that obedience is not something that is required, but something we chose to do."

Bayboo, Erasto, and Tashi were amazed by the vast amount of information they found on the internet. They searched for information about the mysterious manuscript of faith that they were looking for, hoping to find some answers to their questions. They stumbled on a website on faith. "Look at this, Erasto," Bayboo said.

"What is it, Bayboo? Have you found something that we can use?" Erasto asked.

"I stumbled on a website that claimed to have a guide to faith. It's called, Faith Chapter 3, a complete walkthrough," Bayboo said.

They clicked it, curious to see what it was.

They quickly realized that it was not a guide to faith, but a guide to a video game called, "Faith." The game was about a priest who had to exorcise ghosts and demons from a haunted house. The website had detailed instructions on how to complete the game, along with screen shots and videos.

They were confused and disappointed. They didn't understand what this game had to do with faith. "Bayboo, is this some kind of joke?" Erasto asked.

They decided to look for something else. Bayboo typed in "adventure quests" in the search bar hoping to find something more relevant. The search brought up Horace, the famous monkey king, who had many adventures in Totem Ville.

"There is information about a cartoon show based on the characters in the story. This website has summaries of episodes, pictures of the characters, and links to watch the show online," Bayboo said.

The trio were intrigued by what they learned about the show.

"Maybe we can learn something more from the stories of Horace and his friends," Erasto said.

They decided to watch an episode. They clicked the link and watched the show. They were intrigued as Horace and his friends' solved mysteries, puzzles, and situations in Totem Ville. They saw how they helped each other, learned from their mistakes, and had fun along the way.

After the show Erasto said, "I like the characters and enjoyed the show."

"Woof, woof," barked Tashi.

"I liked the animation and the music," Bayboo said. "Did you feel as connected to the story as I did," Bayboo asked, as he recalled their own adventures and challenges?

Erasto nodded his head.

"I wonder if this is what faith is: an unseen substance of joy, friendship, and curiosity. A way of living, learning, and exploring. A sense of wonder, gratitude, and hope," Bayboo said.

They decided to watch another episode. They clicked on the link and watched the show. They laughed and smiled as they watched the characters hold fast to their values and solve the challenges facing them. As they watched, they shared a happy, peaceful feeling.

Although they didn't know it, they had found faith. Not in a book, a game, or a website, but in themselves, each other, and in the world around them. They found faith in their own adventures.

"It is everything we hoped for, although we couldn't see it," Bayboo smiled.

IX

Temperance (Self-Control)

After they had returned to their village from their last quest, Bayboo saw that Erasto was not himself in a fundamental way. He lacked self-control. "It is time for you, Tashi, and I to go on a quest for self-control," he said.

Bayboo, Erasto, and Tashi had been walking for hours in the desert, following a map that the Source of Kindness had given them. They were searching for the Cave of Temptation, where they hoped to find the secret of self-control. The map said the cave was hidden behind a large rock formation, shaped like a camel's hump.

They finally reached the rocks and saw a narrow opening that led to the cave. They entered cautiously, holding a torch to light their way. The cave was dark and damp, and they heard strange noises echoing from the depths. They followed a narrow path that seemed to go deeper and deeper into the earth.

Suddenly, they came across a large chamber filled with all kinds of treasure. There were piles of golden coins, sparkling jewelry, and precious objects. There was also delicious food, exotic clothes, and rare books. The trio were amazed at the sight. They felt a strong urge to take some of the treasure for themselves.

"Wow, look at all this stuff," Bayboo shouted. "We could be rich and famous if we took some of these things, Erasto."

"Yeah. And look at that food!" Erasto exclaimed. "It smells so good, and I'm starving."

"Woof, woof," Tashi barked at the books as if to say, "They must have so much knowledge and wisdom in them."

Just as they were about to grab some of the treasure, they heard a voice from behind them.

"Welcome to the Cave of Temptation, dear strangers," the voice said. "You have come to the right place. Here you can have anything you want. All you do is take it. Go ahead, don't be shy. It's all yours."

They turned around and saw a man standing at the entrance of the chamber. He was handsome and tall, with a charming smile and friendly expression. He wore a white robe, and a golden crown, and held a staff in his hand.

"Who are you?" Bayboo asked.

"I am the keeper of this cave," the man said. "I am here to help you find what you are looking for. You are looking for self-control, right?"

"Yes, we are," Erasto said. "But how can we find it here?"

"It is simple," the man said. "You must pass a test of your will power. This cave is full of temptations. Temptations that appeal to your desires and passions. If you can resist them, then you will prove that you have self-control. If you can't, you will fail and lose everything."

"What do you mean, lose everything," Bayboo asked?

The man smiled and said, "You will see. But don't worry, it is not that hard. You just have to say no to temptation. No to the gold, no to the food, no to the rare books. No to anything that distracts you from your Goal. Can you do that?"

Bayboo, Erasto, and Tashi looked at each other—unsure. They felt the strong pull of the treasure, but also remembered why they had come to the cave. They wanted to learn self-control, not give into their impulses. They wanted to be better people, not greedy and selfish.

They nodded and said, "Yes, we can do that. We can say no to the temptations."

"Very well," the man said. "Then let the test begin. Follow me, and I will show you the way to the next chamber and the challenge that will determine your fate. Are you ready?"

"Yes, we are ready," Bayboo and Erasto said. "Woof," barked Tashi.

They followed the man, leaving the chamber of treasure behind. They hoped that they had made the right choice. They hoped they had enough self-control to pass the test. They hoped they would find the secret they were looking for.

The man led Bayboo, Erasto, and Tashi into the next chamber, which was much smaller than the previous one. There was only one thing in the chamber: a large mirror hanging from the wall.

"This is the final challenge," the man said. "The mirror of truth. It will show you your deepest desire, your true self. If you accept it, you will pass the test. If you can't, then you fail."

"What do you mean, accept it?" Bayboo asked.

"You will see," the man said. "Go ahead, and look into the mirror, one by one. And tell me what you see."

Bayboo went first. He looked into the mirror ands saw himself as a famous musician, playing his guitar on a big stage, with thousands of fans cheering for him. He had always wanted to be a rock star, to express himself through music, to make people happy.

He turned to the man and said, "I see myself as a musician. This is my deepest desire."

"Yes, it is," the man said. "Do you accept it?"

Bayboo hesitated. He wanted to say yes, to embrace his dream, to live his fantasy, but he also remembered why he had come to the cave. He wanted to learn self-control, not chase fame and fortune. He wanted to be humble, not arrogant. He wanted to be real, not fake.

He shook his head and said, "No, I don't accept it. This is not who I really am. This is not who I wish I were. But I know that being a musician is not easy. It takes hard work, dedication, and passion. It also comes with challenges, risks, and sacrifice. I can't just pretend that everything is perfect. I must face reality. I must be myself."

"Very well," said the man. "You have passed the first part of the test. You have resisted the temptation of the mirror. You have shown self-control. Now it is Erasto's turn."

Erasto went next. He looked into the mirror and saw himself as a wealthy entrepreneur, wearing a suit and tie, holding a briefcase full of money. He felt a sense of pride and satisfaction. He had always wanted to be rich, to have a lot of money, to buy everything he wanted.

He turned to the man and said, "I see myself as an entrepreneur, conducting business all over the world. A successful, powerful, influential person that's highly respected. This is my deepest desire."

"Yes, it is," the man said. "Do you accept it?"

Erasto hesitated. He wanted to say yes, to enjoy his wealth, to live in luxury. But he also remembered why he had come to the cave. He wanted to learn self-control, not to be greedy and selfish. He wanted to be generous, not stingy. He wanted to be happy, not materialistic.

He shook his head and said, "No, I don't accept it. This isn't who I really am. This is who I think I should be, but I know that being rich isn't everything. It doesn't guarantee happiness, peace, or love. It also comes with problems, stress, and responsibility. I can't just ignore the needs of others. I must share what I have. I must be grateful."

"Very well," the man said. "You have passed the second part of the test. You have shown self-control. You have resisted the temptation of the mirror. Now it's Tashi's turn."

Tashi went last. He looked into the mirror and saw himself as a human, wearing jeans and a pullover, holding a book in his hand. He felt a sense of curiosity and wonder. He had always wanted to be human, to speak their language, learn their culture, their history.

He turned to the man, who heard Tashi say in his mind, "I see myself as a human being. A smart, educated, knowledgeable human. This is my deepest desire."

"Yes, it is," the man said. "Do you accept it?"

Tashi hesitated. He wanted to say yes, to explore the human world, to learn new things. But he also remembered why he had come to the cave. He wanted to learn self-control, not to be envious and dissatisfied. He wanted to be proud, not ashamed. He wanted to be loyal, and faithful.

He shook his head, and the man heard him say," No, I do not accept it. This is not who I really am. This is who I wish I could be, but I know that being human is not better than being a dog. It has its own advantages and disadvantages. It also comes with expectations, limitations, and conflicts. I can't just abandon my friends. I must stick with them. I must be myself."

"Very well," the man said. "You have passed the final part of the test. You have shown self-control. You have resisted the temptation of the mirror. You have all passed the test. Congratulations, my friends. You have found the secret to self-control.

"What is it?" Bayboo, Erasto, and Tashi asked.

The man smiled and said, "The secret to self-control is to know yourself. To know your strengths and weaknesses, your hopes and fears, your values, and goals. To know what you want and what you need, what you can and what you can't, what you should and what you shouldn't. To know when to say yes and when to say no, when to act and when to wait, when to follow and when to lead. To know yourself is to control yourself. To control yourself is to be free.

"Wow! That is amazing," Bayboo said.

"Thanks for teaching us this valuable lesson," Erasto said. "Thank you for helping us find ourselves."

"Woof, woof, woof," Tashi barked as if to say, "Thank you for being our guide."

"You're welcome, my friends," the man said. "But remember, this is only the beginning. Self-control is not something that you learn once and forget. It is something that you practice every day. In every situation, in every moment. It is a skill that you develop, a habit that you form, a virtue that you cultivate. It is a lifelong journey, not a destination."

"We will, we promise," Bayboo and Erasto said.

"Woof," Tashi barked.

They hugged the man and thanked him. Then they left the cave, feeling happy and fulfilled that they had learned the secret of self-control. They had found themselves. They had completed their quests.

THE END